Then *&* **Now**

ROSNEATH &
THE GARELOCH

Ferry Inn, Rosneath.

BLOOMFIELD, GARELOCHHEAD

Shire Road, Garelochhead.

Then & Now

ROSNEATH &
THE GARELOCH

KEITH HALL

All money raised by the sale of this book will be donated to Rosneath Primary School.

TEMPUS

Gareloch, looking south.

First published 2002
Copyright © Keith Hall, 2002

Tempus Publishing Limited
The Mill, Brimscombe Port,
Stroud, Gloucestershire, GL5 2QG
www.tempus-publishing.com

ISBN 0 7524 2389 4

TYPESETTING AND ORIGINATION BY
Tempus Publishing Limited
PRINTED IN GREAT BRITAIN BY
Midway Colour Print, Wiltshire

Contents

Acknowledgements

I would like to thank the following people for their help and assistance in compiling this book. First and foremost my wife Hilary, for her encouragement, help and endless cups of tea; the staff of Paper Clip, Helensburgh, particularly Alisdair and Darren, for their patience and expertise in reproducing the majority of photographs used in this book; Mrs Ellen Milgrew for typing the bulk of the manuscript; and my daughter, Joanne, for typing the missing bits. I am particularly indebted to my son, Keith, for taking all the 'now' pictures.

I am also grateful to the following for the loan of their photographs: Mr E. Montgomery, Mr and Mrs D. Payne and Mr and Mrs D. Royal.

Finally, I ask for forgiveness of any contributors who may have been unintentionally omitted from these acknowledgements.

Introduction

In 1857 Mr C.W. Maughan, writer, traveller and banker, made a journey, familiar to many of us, around the Gareloch and the Rosneath Peninsular. He recorded his travels in the book, *The Annals of Garelochside*. He tells of a more serene time when the main method of transport was the paddle steamer (the Gareloch had eight piers at this time) or walking.

I have used Mr Maughan's own words to illustrate this journey, his words are more appropriate than those of someone who grew up on a diet of J.T. Edison books and Royal Naval reference manuals. As Mr Maughan wrote: 'It would need all the word painting of a Ruskin to do justice to such a scene', so that's me out of the race. When Mr Maughan refers to 'sixty years ago' he is referring to the late 1700s.

Where possible the 'now' pictures have been taken from the same position as the original ones, and I'm sure Mr Maughan would be grateful to see that his 'lofty' trees are now even more 'lofty'. But, despite the many changes in the area, I cannot help but feel that he would not be totally lost in the 'now' Garelochside and with, perhaps, one or two exceptions, he would approve of the changes made in the district.

A reviewer for the *British Weekly* wrote: 'This is a pleasant book, of a kind that should be multiplied. It makes delightful reading, and its tone is so genial that one cannot but feel kindly to the author.' I for one agreed and perhaps next time you make the journey you will see it through different eyes.

Keith Hall
Tumbledown
September 2002

Rosneath Primary School

The school is situated in the centre of the village of Rosneath. The catchment area extends from Clynder, through Rosneath, to the Caravan Park. The buildings were completed in 1967 and provide well-proportioned accommodation for pupils and teachers in Primaries 3 to7 and adjoining hutment for Primaries 1 and 2, plus a playroom.

The roll of the school is presently 157 with a total capacity of 268.

Rosneath Primary recognises the extremely important role of parents in the education of their children and is proud of the strong parental links that have been established. These links are being further developed in partnership with the Homelink Worker. There is also excellent support from the School Board and PTA.

The school enjoys close links with the two village churches and the surrounding village, in particular the Senior Citizens group and the nursery. We welcome all members of the community to our school services, sports days, concerts and coffee afternoons. These links are very important to us in our attempt to provide a well-rounded education for the children in our care. We would like to thank the author of this book, Mr Keith Hall, for his interest in the school, it is very much appreciated.

Mrs Pamela Atack
Head Teacher

Books by the Same Author:

Clyde Submarine Base	0 7524 1657 X
Gareloch and Rosneath Peninsula	0 7524 2106 9
HMS Dolphin: Gosport's Submarine Base	0 7524 2113 1

One
The Parish of Row

Great have been the changes in the appearance of the parish of Row since the year 1830, when the lands began to be feued, and steamers regularly made the voyage from Glasgow to Garelochhead. Starting from the Loch Long end of the parish, there was an old farmhouse with a thatched roof at Finnart and a similar one at Arddarroch, both of which have long since been demolished, while the two modern residences, which are seen amid their surrounding plantations, were built about the year 1830 by Mr Burn the architect. Whistlefield, which stands at the brow of the ridge between Loch Long and the Gareloch, was then a small public house, frequented by drovers, who were conducting cattle to Portincaple, whence they were ferried across Loch Long. They had come by the old drove road which led above Finnart, along the high ground at Garelochhead, always keeping well up the sides of the hill, and avoiding the modern impositions of tolls. Here and there, traces of the old road may yet be seen, but it has long been disused. Portinacaple is a small cluster of cottages where a few fishermen prosecute their calling in the dark waters of Loch Long. Returning to the road which runs down from the brow of the hill to Garelochhead, on the left-hand side, near the burn, are traces of the old meal mill which, long ago, used to stand there, with a few thatched cottages in the vicinity. At the foot of the road, near the shore, is the boundary between Rosneath and Row parish.

The villas which constitute Garelochhead now come into view; the little cottages, tiled or thatched, which in former years sheltered the inhabitants, have nearly all disappeared. Several of the older natives can remember when there were no slated houses at the head of the loch, except Bendarroch, which was built about 1833, and Fernicarry. Some old cottages used to stand at the entrance to Bendarroch, and a few others near the Inn, which, fifty years ago, was a three-storey house, and, after being burnt down, was built in its present form. Just beyond the Inn there was formerly the Tollhouse, a small public house, one of the numerous humble hostelries where whisky used to be dispensed to all and sundry. On holidays the *Waverley*, *James Oswald* or *Clarence* would bring numbers of excursionists, who were landed either by the ferryboat or sometimes in the steamer's own boat, for there were no piers in those days and the steamer had to be made fast to a buoy.

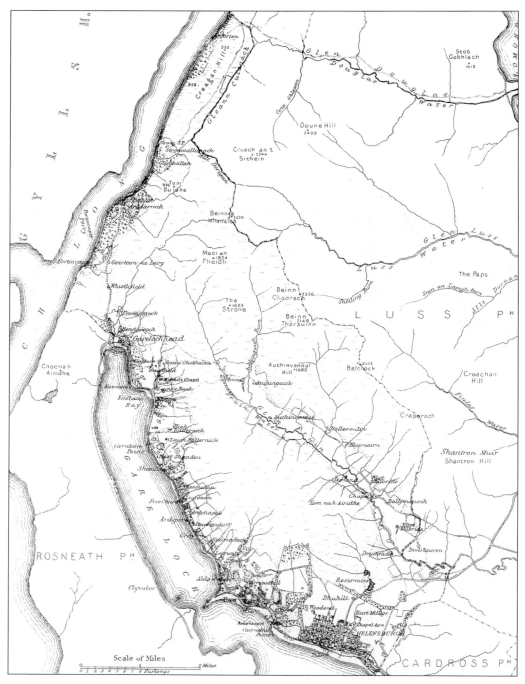

A map of the old Row parish. The spelling was changed to Rhu in 1927.

The railway station at Whistlefield; the entrance to Loch Goil can be seen in the distance.

Whistlefield.

Walking along the shore you pass the pier, built in 1845 on nineteen years lease by Mr McFarlane, so long the tenant of Faslane. In former years there were good large sailing boats, owned by Archibald Niven, that took passengers and goods both from Garelochhead, Rosneath and Row over to Greenock. Faslane bay is soon reached, and here the sides of the loch are well wooded, with grassy slopes leading up to the heather hills above and handsome villas are seen gleaming amid their surrounding plantations. Faslane House, the former residence of the Macaulays, and latterly of the Colquhouns of Luss, is a little way back from the middle of the bay. A good way down from the house, near the shore, there stands the old oak tree under whose boughs, according to tradition, the crowing of a cock presaged the death of a Macaulay. The name of the spot Cnoch-na-Cullah, or 'Knoll of the Cock', seems appropriate to the legend. Faslane is an irregular pile, the front having been built in 1863, the portion behind about 1745, and a still older small structure at the rear.

There is a rolling stream, with many a dark eddying pool and foaming cascade, which runs past the house into the peaceful bay. In former years the Colquhouns of Luss lived at Faslane for a short time in summer as a sort of marine residence, occupying the older part of the mansion.

The present tenant of Faslane is Mr John McFarlane, who is now at an advanced age, and during this long residence on the Gareloch he has gained the regard of all who know his eminence as an agriculturist, and his worth as a man. His grandfather came to Faslane in 1785 from Glenfruin and three generations of the family have tenanted the farm, with other holdings in Glenfruin and Arrochar. Mr McFarlane can give many interesting reminiscences of his lifelong connection with the district, and the changes that he has seen on the shores of the Gareloch. When he was a boy, all along the loch until you came to Ardencaple Castle, there were only thatched cottages here and there, with the exception of Ardenconnell and three or four farmhouses. In his early days nearly every farmer grew flax, which went through several processes on the farm, except heckling, which was done in Greenock. The flax came back to be spun in the house, and then was sent to the weaver to be made into linen. The 'lint dub', as it was called, was a circular pool of water near Faslane House, in which the lint was steeped and afterwards dried on the grass. In those days the wages of the farm servants were less than a half of what they now receive, sticks were gathered in the woods for fuel, and the old fashioned 'cruisie' gave a feeble light. Rude candles, with rashes for wicks, were manufactured out of sheep fat; there were no butchers, not even in Helensburgh, and the farmers killed their own beef and mutton. In summer the lambs were killed, and in autumn several families would join together in laying in the supply of salted meat usually provided by the farmers from their cattle. Salt was heavily taxed for common use, but no duty was levied on the salt used for curing herring, and the salt car regularly appeared in the herring season.

Letters delivered by post were few and far between, and the postman carried his bag between Helensburgh and Garelochhead – a duty latterly performed by the well-known 'Jenny the Post'. Shops on the lochside were almost unknown, but there was one at Shandon, kept by Mrs Comrie, for sale of teas, tobacco and groceries, brought by the carrier's carts. Occasionally bread came from Helensburgh in vans, and the steamers landed small wares and stores in the ferryboats. There was a smith's shop at Helensburgh, and one at Garelochhead for the requirements of the wide district. The schoolmaster at Garelochhead – Bain by name – resided in Helensburgh and made his perambulations to and fro, and, being addicted to botany, frequently used to diverge from the road, to the detriment of the expectant children. At Rowmore there was a character known as 'the sodger' who lived in one of the thatched cottages, while the old toll-house at the head of what is now Balernock pier used to sell spirits, being a favourite 'howff' for the aforesaid man-of-war and others in quest of alcoholic conviviality and the libations of 'mountain dew', often leading to hilarious uproar.

There is still living in Dumbarton, in his ninety-second year, Mr John Bell, who, along with his father, has for many years been a cattle salesman in the county and frequently visited the Gareloch. The old drove roads in Dunbartonshire and neighbouring counties were well known to him, though now most of them have been long since disused, and their grass-grown track can scarcely be distinguished amid the heather and bracken. Many a time has he been around the Gareloch, and driven cattle across the Rosneath peninsula, transacting business with those famed agriculturists, Lorne Campbell of Portkill, Long Chamberlain of Argyll, and Buchanan of Ardenconnell. Eighty years ago it was a work of some difficulty to transport a large drove of

The Clachan at Loch Long.

The Gareloch from above Garelochhead.

The village smithy.

sheep from Argyllshire to Carman market, near Dumbarton, but the drovers had ample time at their disposal, and had plenty of friends to see. In those days the old Lennox territory on the Gareloch, most of which is now adorned with handsome villas and smiling gardens garlanded with flowers, was a bare stretch of heath-clad pastures, with an occasional thatched cottage indicating the presence of inhabitants. About the year 1818 Mr Bell took part in one of the old-fashioned conventicles, on a Sabbath day, near Garelochhead, where there were then a few scattered buildings. The Cameronian minister of Kilmalcolm, whose name was McLauchlan had procured the old Dumbarton steamer, and a contingent of persons joined at Helensburgh, Dumbarton and other places, the preaching 'tent' being set up on a hillside commanding a fine view of the loch. The day turned out very wet, but having been announced several days before, there was a numerous company, though the impression left upon Mr Bell's mind was that the proceedings partook rather too much of a scene of conviviality and excitement, by no means of a spiritual character.

Smuggling was extensively carried on: many a still was in full swing, and Mr Bell can recall some of the incidents when the officers of Excise, accompanied by dragoons, proceeded on their mission of investigation. Even some of the farmers in the county practised this demoralising trade, and, on one occasion, a well-known innkeeper on the lochside liquidated a debt owing by him by proceeding to his garden and digging in the ground, where a cask of fine, old smuggled whisky was disinterred. In Dumbarton the smugglers who had been caught in their operations used to be confined, often for weeks at a time, in the old Tolbooth in the High Street, nearly opposite the Elephant Hotel. Here those awaiting their trial contrived to pass a pleasant enough time and, after being divided into messes of five, one would act in his turn as cook, and excellent broth, beef and potatoes could be prepared in the comfortable room, in which at each end were two large fireplaces. Whisky was also procured from the outer world by means of a string, to which a stocking was attached containing an empty bottle, being lowered from the window and hauled up again with the requisite supply of the national beverage. With a complaisance only too common, the jailer winked at these proceedings and was even known, at a time, to leave the door of the prison unlocked so that the beleaguered inmates could enjoy a short outing by way of relief to the monotony of their enforced sojourn. All along the shores of the Gareloch there were glens in which smuggling went on. Under cover of night the casks of whisky would be stowed safely in small boats which were able to get up the mouth of the burns, and from thence the contraband article was rowed away and landed under the Castle Rock of Dumbarton, or possibly taken to Greenock and distributed among the various inns and public houses. There are still one or two old men living on the Garelochside who have similar tales to tell, but few have their memories so alert and vivid as the aged tenant of Faslane who, from his windows, can command a fine view over the loch and the hillside on which his long life has been so happily spent.

Crossing to the burn at the back of Faslane House, the old burying place, round the picturesque ruins of the ancient chapel, is seen on the slope of the field. It is a sequestered and beautiful spot, with oak and ash trees throwing their shade over the mouldering walls, all mantled with wallflowers and creepers, and the upper end of the enclosure is rank with long grass. An ash tree of some size has long grown within the crumbling walls, and spread its great boughs over the ruins, while the roofless structure offers free entrance to wintry gales and summer zephyrs alike, with rushing wailing sounds. Thorns and briars protrude their encroaching roots from the lower parts of the wall, and a mournful air of forlorn solitude pervades the scene. Here and there, concealed by the long tufted grass, a moss-covered stone indicates where repose the remains of those laid at rest, centuries ago, in this lonesome field. Tender memories, doubtless appealing to many, hover round this silent house of the dead, and in the calm summer evening, towards the witching hour of night, the sweet lay of the mavis resounds amid the ruins. The erection of Faslane chapel, apparently of most uncertain antiquity, may date from the rise of the family of Lennox, whose piety was undoubted, as was their munificence as donors of property to the early church. Under their auspices, the chapel of St Michael may have aided in diffusing the light of the Gospel throughout the surrounding country.

Cottages at the foot of Whistlefield Brae.

Benarroch Bend, Garelochhead.

The village as seen from the railway station.

A little way beyond, passing by some grey and gnarled beeches and an old drying kiln near the murmuring stream, while the field slopes steeply up to the moor, the site of the ancient stronghold or castle of Faslane is reached. It lies in a wooded glen, at the junction of two fern-fringed, mossy-banked burns, amid the oak coppice that clothes the glen and conceals its windings, until it is lost in the abrupt declivity of the hills. When you come to the spot, small dark pools of water are seen gathering at the foot of the miniature cascades, which conduct the stream over gleaming facets of slaty rock. Where the two burns meet there is a mound, now thickly clad with trees, which is supposed to be the site of the former abode of the old Lords of Lennox. From this there is a fine view of the Gareloch and its verdant shores, with the leafy promontories at its lower end, and the quiet bay of Faslane in the foreground. Nothing now remains in the vicinity of the once formidable keep to show that here stood a tower of strength and place of warlike defence, against the beleaguering foes who might cluster upon the eminences around. It is not easy to conjecture where the large number of retainers, who congregated round the old feudal castles, could well have found their dwellings in the immediate vicinity of Faslane, but the bowmen and men at arms would be in the lower part of the building. The rest of the men who turned out on warlike occasions would no doubt be armed with target and broadsword, for it must be remembered that in those early days there was little wealth in Scotland, and few could indulge in the splendour of a complete suit of armour. The steel bonnet and leather jacket were common and the breast-plate would be of armour, while after the sixteenth century firearms came into play, and hagbuts, harquebusses, culverins and pistolets formed part of the defensive covering worn by warriors. This secluded glen must have resounded with the warlike clangour of the mustering followers of the proud Earls of Lennox, and where now the peaceful swain tends his flocks and herds, there would be seen the armed bands of the chief, gathering round the long silken pennant of war as it fluttered in the breeze.

From the moor above the glen of Faslane there is an easy ascent to the summit of Mhaol-na-Fheidh, which rises to a height of 1,934ft above the loch and the equivalent of which in English is 'round hill of the deer'. No doubt the easier and more direct road up to the summit is from the village of Garelochhead, commencing the ascent from beyond the railway station. Very soon you find yourself on the springy heather, after passing some rough grassy stretches, thickly covered in parts with rushes and bog myrtle. Here and there will be noticed some of the ice boulders which are encountered in this locality, one in particular, is deeply grooved with glacial marks on its surface. Birch trees cover the lower glades of the hill and traces of an old drove road may be seen, while an occasional shirr of the grouse or cry of the moor cock falls upon the ear as the birds are startled from their repose. After a time the climb becomes more arduous and one rounded height succeeds another until, not far from the top, there is a stretch of peat hagg strewn with shells and white quartzose stones. Then a steep grassy face leads up to the summit and from its broad eminence there is a grand view over the adjacent valley and surrounding mountains.

A far-reaching and varied prospect is gained both over the Gareloch district and away to the distant confines of Perthshire in one direction, with the remoter islands beyond Argyllshire in the other, and Loch Long and Glenfruin at your feet: a grand expanse of mountain, moor, loch and heathery glade, steep corries and boulder strewn glens. Specially striking are the lofty,

The village from the hill above the railway station.

BLOOMFIELD, GARELOCHHEAD

Garelochhead looking south.

jagged peaks of Arran and Mull, the former looming dark and shadowy against the skyline, while the rugged outline of Mull seems like a solid mass of dense purple clouds. On some of the distant peaks the sun rays are sleeping, giving a pyramid of light against the encircling shade, while others are scarce seen in their gloomy sublimity amid the haze of the horizon. Gleams of bright lustre indicate the smooth lake with its silvery strand and waving woods of dark firs clothe the rounded outlines of the lesser heights. Right down below there are the steep pastoral slopes, dotted with sheep, that rise from the winding Glen Macarn, lonely and green, the road leading towards Luss showing like a narrow thread in the quiet valley. It meets the upper reaches of Glenfruin, whose lower part blends with the meadow lands on the banks of the river. Loch Lomond is partly descried, from Luss towards its southern end, and the islands that chequer the calm waters of this beautiful loch. Balmaha with its craggy sides and rocky heights shows across the loch, the woods around Buchanan, the great expanse of open country towards Stirling and the Ochills. Casting the eye round by Fintry and the high hills in that direction, the glance rests upon the shores of the Clyde in all their beauty. Ardmore, that dusky headland, stands out, with the fainter outline of Dumbarton rock beyond, and on the opposite point is Rosneath Castle and grounds with a gleaming stretch of water between. Only the lower part of the Gareloch is visible from the summit, but the long unbroken ridge of the Rosneath peninsula, intervenes between the former loch and Loch Long, with two shining patches of water on the higher ground.

Away towards the Cowal mountains, round the Holy Loch and Dunoon, there is more of shadow and Bute and the Cumbraes seem blended together in a mass of darkening haze. Through a gap in the ranges of Loch Goil, there emerges the crest of Ben Cruachan and the grey granite crags of that stern landscape tell of its desolate wildness. Sweeping round by the high peaks, near the head of Glenfalloch, Ben More, Ben Lui, Ben Ledi and mighty Ben Lawers are standing in isolated grandeur. There is that sense of freedom and vastness which an extended view, such as this, yields to the lonely spectator, who surveys from his coign of

24

vantage a sight so noble and diversified. The name of this hill shows that apparently, at one time, the deer had ranged up and down these deep glens and wooded straths, but they have long ceased to frequent these heights and the valleys are given up to sheep and cattle.

Beneath the dark shadows of some of these stately peaks, towering over the undulating country below, strange scenes have been enacted and the memory kindles at the thought of many moving deeds. What from afar seems a hollow, wreathed in blue mist, placid and undisturbed, long centuries ago witnessed an awful struggle amid the din of clan warfare and the riot of predatory foray. Beneath these distant precipices there sleeps the dark tarn, over whose coldly gleaming surface the lambent sunlight rarely plays. Perchance the suicide's despairing frame may have sunk to dreary repose beneath the icy wave, as with desperate resolve he plunged into those depths that gave not up their dead. While but a little way down the unfrequented valley, past winding meads bordered by mossy sward, gay with flowers and spangled with iridescent dewdrops, beneath ivied towers and vernal groves of clustering trees, there leaps joyously to the ocean a sparkling, foaming river. Lightly floating amid the evening breeze, the airy gossamer flings its filmy tissue over the quivering tendrils of the tiny harebell and wild sweet briar. Fine pictorial effects of alternate light and shade are seen on some of the bracken-circled lochs, as the sunlight falls upon grey streaks of rocky veins, blended with softer knolls of grass and fern, while the white sail of a solitary yacht for a moment arrests the eye.

Returning to Faslane bay, the house known as Belmore appears in the midst of a flourishing plantation, near the road. There stood, in the early part of the century, two thatched houses at the turn of the bay in front of Rowmore and others at Chapelton, near the old church, some of

The village.

Garelochead Pier.

Looking north.

which were inhabited by weavers and others by farm-labourers. One of those at Belkmore was the abode of a noted smuggler, Cambell by name, and indeed, too many of the cottagers were addicted to this illicit but fascinating employment. There was a public house beside an old ash tree on the shore side of the road, which was said at one time to have been kept by a descendant of the Macaulays of Ardencape. Belmore was originally built soon after 1830 by a fisherman of the name of McFarlane, and was a small two-storey house, while some years it was afterwards was sold to Mr Honeyman, who added considerably to the plain structure. Subsequently it was acquired in 1856 by Mr McDonald who remodelled the mansion, giving it the handsome appearance that it now has. In those days the loch side presented a wild scene of nature – whins, sloes, wild roses and the indigenous copse woods and shrubs of the district, abounded on the hillside, with a few older trees and belts of plantations on the farms. Meikle and Laigh Balernock, Letrualt, Blairvaddick and Torr, the farms that succeed one another on the way to Helensburgh, then showed none of the modern villa-residences that now are planted on their lands. West Shandon, where now the palatial Hydropathic establishment stands, was then a small cottage, added to by the eminent Robert Napier, who purchased it and reared the fine Gothic mansion, so well-known as the residence for many years of that pioneer of the famous Clyde shipbuilders. Shandon House, which lies beyond, was, fifty years ago, a plain, substantial structure which had been built as a summer residence on a lease of 319 years by Mr Ogilvie of Carron, and had over forty acres of land attached. Afterwards, the late Walter Buchanan, so genial and popular, and who for a number of years so worthily represented Glasgow in Parliament, lived at Shandon, which had been burnt down and rebuilt in its present tasteful architectural form.

The earliest of the villas at Shandon was Linburn, built in the1940s by Samuel McCall, well known as an honourable Glasgow merchant, and also esteemed as a good deal of a 'character' by the dwellers on that side of the Gareloch. His white silk stockings, old-fashioned stock, long-tailed coat, and carefully starched ruffles bespoke the old beau of bygone years, so dear to the caricaturists of the early Victorian days, and his cuisine had gained a reputation which was

The remains of the chapel in Faslane cemetery.

29

Vista, just south of Faslane Bay.

Belmore House.

Balernock House.

The Shadon Hydorpathic Hotel – former home of Robert Napier.

confirmed by the aristocratic proprietor and guests at Ardencaple Castle. The old gentleman was very particular in the straight line of his avenue, the formation of his walls, and the symmetry of his garden. A little previous to this, the villa known as Berriedale, now occupied as a 'Home' for poor children, had been built by a Macaulay, and subsequently bought by Mr Sinclair of the Caithness family, who named it after the title of the eldest son of that ancient house. It is on the shore, between the road and the beach, on a narrow strip of ground, and Mr Sinclair began, though he did not finish, both Croy and Broomfield, now conspicuous among the villas on that side of the loch. Above this, on the hillside, is seen the large mansion of Blairvaddick, which at first was an old-fashioned, square, two-storey house with attics, and was enlarged by James Buchanan of Ardenconnell, who resided there. The late Sir James Anderson, who reared the existing structure, pulled it down in the 1960s. Fiunnery, where lived the well-known family of Macleods who have given so many eminent scions to the Church of Scotland, is one of the prettily embowered villas on the Shandon shore, and was the loved abode of Dr Norman Macleod. Broomieknowe and Altdonaig, near the entrance to the 'Whistlers Glen', are passed as you approach Row, the former being where Sir James Watson resided; he was an esteemed citizen of Glasgow and latterly its civic head. The two houses at one time formed the dwelling and part of the extensive buildings of a large company of distillers, and many a cargo of malt liquors has been taken from the little cove that used to be at the mouth of the burn. The existing house of Altdonaig was for a time, when it had ceased to be occupied as a malt house, the place in which the early Free Church congregation assembled for worship, in the stirring 'Disruption' days. James Glen, the joiner and crofter of that period, built the middle portion of Broomieknowe, and the distillery was known as Altdunnalt. The colas, barrels, stores of malt, and other requisites all used to be landed at the mouth of the burn, which was sufficiently enlarged to admit boats lying there at high water. At the back of Altdunnalt was a row of workmens houses, and two other cottages stood near the road a little to the west of Broomiknowe, along with the house, shop, and stable of one of the proprietors of the distillery. At the back of the cottages was an old, never-failing spring of water, and farther on was another well, known familiarly as the 'Clash Well' from the fact of its being a place of resort for the gossips of this now bygone hamlet. A little nearer Row as an eminence, a green bank above the strand, well-clad with grass and known as the 'shelling hill', from the fact of the farmers and crofters sometimes, in fine weather, winnowing their grain at this point.

From this height easy access is gained to the romantic glen, formerly called Aldonalt, from the Dualt burn which runs through the glen; a rugged gorge full of birch, fir, ash, oak and hazel trees. It is easy to gain the summit of the glen by keeping above its shelving banks, and peering down through the overhanging trees the silvery stream is seen glancing over its slaty bed, frequently gathered in deep pools, overhung with mossy stones and steep breasts of rock. Every now and then a fine peep is gained of the Gareloch, hemmed in with its tree-covered slopes and its background of rounded hills, the long tongue of gravel at Row forming a barrier to the splashing waves. When you descend into the leafy recesses of the glen and look upwards and downwards at its sinuous course, its romantic beauties must strike the wanderer in this cool retreat from the hot sunshine of a long summer day. On all sides its steep, mossy and grassy banks are gay with the flowers which, in their seasons, adorn the spot: primroses, violets, bluebells, hyacinths, honeysuckle and many varieties of ferns, mosses and ivy. A delightful spot for the artist or lover of nature, for the combination of rippling waterfall, glistening rocks, and long leafy vistas of tender, green undergrowth, offer innumerable subjects for the artist. In addition to the beauties with which the bountiful hand of nature has embellished the glen, it has a legend for the lovers of fancy lore. A woman in grey, visible when the moon is at its full and hanging over a dark linn at the head of the valley, where it emerges from the moor, is said to be heard sometimes moaning, to the sad accompaniment of the fitful night breeze, over her long-lost lover whose body was found close to the haunted pool.

This glen was, in former days, the scene of a considerable industry of slate quarrying, and the old roads for carrying away the slates can be distinctly traced on both sides of the stream. The

...........and how it looks today.

Shandon Church.

refuse from the workings fills many parts of the hollow, and old faces, where the slate was cut, are seen on the slopes of the glen. One of the last of the workers lived in a sort of natural cavern, which he managed to form into a rude house, or 'bourach', the site of which is to be seen. He was known as Duncan 'of the bourach', from his place of abode, and here he lived and brought up his family. At the spot known as the 'tongue of the glen', where the Ardenconnell and Succoth glens meet, there is a great heap of debris from the slate works. Parts of the latter glen are very steep and rocky, and the unseen stream is heard rippling over its pebbly bed far below. The visitor is rewarded for his exploring of the Succoth glen by beautiful bits of scenery, and, if he knows where to look for them, harts tongue, lady fern and other less common species will reward his search. This place was a favourite site for smuggling operations, and before the railway cutting had interfered with the seclusion of the glen, there was to be seen one of the complete, built-in stills and fire places, where the illicit work was carried on. The curious thing was that it was not thought criminal or disreputable to engage in this contraband trade sixty years ago. It was quite customary for young men to hire themselves out to smugglers for six months, just like farm servants at a feeing market. On one occasion the dragoons captured a large barrel of whisky and lodged it in an outhouse at the Row Inn. While they went inside to

Kirkpatrick Lane, Rhu.

Shandon Pier.

Rhu Pier, now the marina.

enjoy a refresher for the journey to Dumbarton, the smugglers ran off all the whisky by starting a hoop and substituted water in the barrel, after which they got clear away and the theft was only discovered when the contraband goods came to be examined.

On the farm of Torr, in a plantation near the Succoth glen, there is to be seen probably the last remaining smugglers still, in situ, all just as it was left, when used in the 1940s. The place for the water barrel is surrounded by large stones where the malt was steeped beside the still, and the tunnel for the smoke, leading from the fireplace, is over 12ft long, the very stones showing traces of fire. All are in a wonderful state of preservation considering the rude and hasty way in which the smugglers erected their plant. Up above this wood, where the field joins on to the moor, there are some sweet, secluded spots: hollows carpeted with the finest turf and their mossy banks scenting the air with wild thyme and violets; white saxifrage overspreading the velvety turf, primroses, bluebells, meadow sweet and a bright parterre of wild flowers.

On the side of the 'Whistler's Glen' nearest to Row is the fine old wood surrounding Ardenconnell House, a solid plain mansion of grey-coloured stone, built more than a century ago by Mr Andrew Buchanan. It has a fine commanding position and from its front there is a wide prospect of mountain, moor and loch. The beech and oak trees are of great size and give an air of antiquity and dignity to the old mansion, which is a conspicuous object in the landscape, as seen from this point. In former days the Ardenconnell garden used to run down as far as the field at the back of the church, and the tracks of the walks of the garden are distinctly marked on the field. No houses were then built on Row point, which was covered with turf and afforded good pasture for cows. Passing by the old church of Row and the few red-tiled cottages facing the green, the Inn appears, with the building known as 'Row House' adjoining, which had been erected by James Buchanan of Ardenconnell, who subsequently lived in it. The whole row of buildings, as they now face Row bay, with the exception of the substitution of slates for red tiles, look much as they did in the early part of the century, but two or three thatched cottages, which stood where Inchalloch gate is now, have disappeared. The road was a rough track, thickly bordered with whins, brambles and wild roses. Passing what used to be known as 'Spy's lane', after one of that name whose family has long occupied a respectable position in the Row district, the view opened up of Cairndhu point, with Rosneath bay opposite and the promontory of Ardmore in the distance. None of the handsome villas now nestling amid the leafy slopes of Row were in existence in 1830, for there was no pier. The long avenue, with fine beech trees on either side ending where the pier now stands, led up to Ardenconnell, the only mansion until you came to Ardencaple. In 1833 Woodstone was built, and Rowmore, Ardenmore, Dalarne, Rossleas on the point and others followed in rapid succession, until we have now the modern summer resort of Row.

The geologist will find much to reward his glance over the shore and rocks at the point of Row, or Rhue as it was formerly spelt. Even when the tide is nearly at its full, there is generally a strong ripple, sometimes in windy weather a crest of small breakers showing where the long tongue of land projects from the bay over the narrow channel, and giving the Gareloch its placid, inland lake appearance. In all probability, ages ago, the whole Gareloch was filled with a glacier, and its 'terminal' moraine would be where the point now is, and the clay and gravel, which the glacier discharged from its end, gradually formed the natural rampart that almost bars the entrance of the sea.

While summer throws its mantle of lovely green over the landscape, still the view from the shingly strand of the Row promontories, in early winter, has also a peculiar charm and beauty. The loch is pervaded by a dull, leaden hue, contrasting with more intensity against the snowy slopes above and the fitful gleams of sunshine lying in patches on the hills beyond Glenfruin. Delicate effects of light and shade are displayed from the sunrays striking upon the rugged ridges

Rhu Pier.

The village of Rhu.

The village of Rhu.

of rock and scaur outlined against the snowy surface beyond. On a sudden, the sun suffuses the misty cloud on the summit of one of the far off peaks, then glints down into the intervening valley and just touches the summits of the mountains above Arrochar, all arrayed in their snowy garb. Near Loch Goil the hills are partly illumined, and partly obscured with gathering shade, while all the lesser heights on the Rosneath shore are lit up by the slanting sunrays, where the bare and skeleton woods streak the undulating slopes. Then are noticed the old furrows far up the hillsides, as the fleecy snow indicates their form; the hedgerows have caught and retained the flakes of snow, and the dark masses of fir are also powdered with the glittering rime. The yellow bracken rises in patches out of the snow, gleaming in russet beauty in the sun, and the fringe of larches and firs on the ridge of the moor, through which the glinting rays of light penetrate, look soft against the background of misty uplands. Some of the fields are bare and destitute of colour, as if the wind had swept them of their wintry covering, while long stretches of sunshine streak the lower part of the hills near Garelochhead, the upper peaks hardly seen in the waning light. In many parts the trunks of trees look gaunt amid the lustrous sheen of the surrounding wintry landscape. Each rough dyke or turf-covered wall seems to stand out in relief against the white surface of the ground around, dark masses of purple heather crown many a swelling height, and a calm pervades the scene. An occasional fling of sunshine rests for a moment on the pale grey boughs of the silver fir and birch, and tips the crests of the topmost trees, while the red, withered leaves of the beech rustle at times in the wintry blast. The glistening, green ivy imparts colour to some of the bare stems of older trees, and the mossy mantle, clinging like an emerald velvet robe to the grey wood, gives additional warm tints.

Sometimes, on a winter morning in December, beautiful effects of light and shade will be observed in the sky, and also in the reaches of water about Row bay, and in the opposite bay of Campsail. Towards the high hills beyond Loch Long the background is misty, but a large opening in the cloudy canopy seems to illumine the sky over Glenfruin. This has a delicate pale grey hue, and is bordered with faintly moving fringes of vaporous clouds, growing brighter and brighter, with delicate streaks of red gleaming athwart the sky, which now begins to show a lovely silvery grey. The water near the shore is of a leaden colour, the dense dark reflections of the trees sleep in the loch, all along the shore of the Mill bay, and the hulls and masts of the boats are black and motionless. The crossing ferryboat casts a sombre shade against the glassy lambent tide, and there is a wondrous play of glistening sheen on the surface of the water. The white seagull, for an instant, poises with tremulous pinion, and then wheels gracefully away, and in the middle channel the circling eddies of the purple water catch the ripple of light. Subtle gradations of silvery lustre, faint violet tints, and subdued greys, all combine to sweet and verdant patches of greensward are passed as, following the sparkling streamlet, the visitor skirts the end of Ardencaple and arrives at the Woodend farm in the west of Helensburgh.

Returning to the cluster of houses which constitutes the village of Row, and standing at the end of the narrow strip of land once known as the 'Ferry Acres', the view has many features of interest. Ferry Acres is now clothed with a plantation of fir trees, in which, a dozen years ago, a colony of rooks established themselves. Rhu Lodge, built early in the century by Lord John Campbell, has lost the picturesque aspect which it used to present when covered over with a thatch of heather. The ferry was a busy scene for days when Carman fair was in the era of its glory. Droves of cattle would come across from Argyllshire, by way of Ardentinny and Rosneath, and horses would cross at Row ferry by the simple process of making them swim over after the ferryboat. On the left hand was the old church and schoolhouse where, among other teachers, taught the unfortunate John Arrol who, in the year 1760, was murdered by a man named Cunningham, who resided in Dumbarton. The murderer confessed that he had paid Arrol the sum of £30, a debt that he owed, and having got a receipt for the money, stabbed his victim to the heart with a knife. After hiding the body for some time in a disused chimney, he took it one dark night to the Leven and sunk it in the stream. Cunningham was suspected from the first of having murdered the poor schoolmaster, and after the body was recovered from the Leven, he was asked to undergo the trial by touch, from the universal belief that if the murderer touched the body of his victim, the wound would bleed afresh. Cunningham, however, declined the ordeal, but his conscience gave him no rest until he had confessed his guilt. Arrol's grave is

Ardenconnel House.

Ardencarple Castle, the west tower can just be seen above the trees.

Ardencarple Castle.

in the south-east corner of the parish churchyard at Dumbarton with the inscription 'Here Lyes the body of John Aroll, schoolmaster, at Ye Row, who Died February the 2nd, 1760, aged 52 years', followed by a Latin inscription.

On the grassy bank below Woodstone, near the shore, those curious in such matters will find a square stone, with a hole cut in the centre and the four sides cut away, to all appearance having once been the socket of an upright beam of wood. Antiquaries have inspected it, gravely advancing theories to account for its peculiar shape, but the most probable and prosaic one is that it was used to support a flag staff set up when the Queen and Prince Albert anchored off Helensburgh in 1847. However, the local gypsies and tinkers used the stone as a sort of washing basin, when the exigencies of their wandering life required such a ceremony. At the head of Row pier, is the entrance to what, for nearly a century, was the avenue gate of Ardenconnell. Formerly it was known as the 'white yett', from the fine-hewn pillars supporting the gate, and old beech and ash trees on either side can be followed all the way up to the mansion. It is now a public road, with villas here and there in the woods adjoining, and is the site of Row pier, a massive structure, built of high blocks of stone, superior in strength and solidity to any similar pier on the Clyde. Here the venerable form of Angus Colquhoun, a splendid specimen of a highlander, is rarely absent from his post on the arrival of the steamers. Angus is known near and far, and invests the familiar minor pier guardians at other Clyde resorts. The 'Lagarie Croft' was the field now occupied by Armadale Villa, and a little way beyond, on the road side, was the row of thatched houses known as the 'Shore houses of Torr', in which lived the labourers on that farm. There used to be a yair opposite Lagarie, and fish have been taken from it less than 60 years ago, but most of the stones were used in building the sea wall below the road, and only a few are left. A little way beyond Lagarie there stands, on the roadside, the old Ardencaple Inn, now a private dwelling house but, at the beginning of the century, a place of resort for travellers posting to and from the Argyllshire Highlands. The Duke of Argyll built it when the old and humble edifice, which did duty as an inn at Cairndhu point, was pulled down and which, for a time, served as the stables for the new inn.

Ardencaple Castle is certainly the most interesting of the old residences on the Gareloch, and stands on a fine site overlooking the entrance to that beautiful sheet of water. The old castle is an irregular pile of buildings placed on a massive foundation, all covered over with thick ivy. Part of the structure dates back to the fourteenth century, but there is not much in the architecture to attract the notice of the antiquary. There are several vaulted chambers, dark and dismal, in the lowest part of the old castle, which probably go back to a very remote date. The fine old trees around the castle give it an ancient look, in harmony with the wooded landscape and moorland background. In front of the castle is the projecting headland known as Cairndhu, where the old inn and outhouses used to stand. It is now known as Kidston Park, from the fact that it was purchased and presented to the town of Helensburgh by members of the family of that name. Helensburgh owes a deep debt of gratitude to the Kidstons, who have resided there for several generations, the first of the family, Richard Kidston, having filled the office of provost of the Burgh in the year 1836. Of his three sons, William, Richard and Charles, the first mentioned was, for many years, a well-known and prominent figure in ecclesiastical, social and political circles – a most generous friend to education, a philanthropist of wide sympathies, and one who wrought incessantly for the good of his fellowmen. Only one member of the family still survives, the friend of the friendless, the gentle and devoted promoter of many Christian works

KIDSTON PARK, HELENSBURGH.

Kidston Park.

Two

The Parish of Rosneath

The beautiful peninsula of Rosneath has long been a favourite place of resort for those who are in search of romantic and salubrious summer quarters. There is a wondrous charm about the sinuous shores and winding bays of the Firth of Clyde, overlooked as they are by many a heathery mountain slope, across whose breezy heights flit the ever changing shadows of a summer day. Last century the scenery of the valley and estuary of the Clyde presented an aspect very different from their now luxuriant clothing of well-tilled lands and spreading plantations. Anyone then sailing along the Clyde saw the heather and bracken-clad slopes of the hills, interspersed with glens, in which the indigenous birch and alder trees grew in profusion, but none of the great plantations of larch, spruce and silver firs, which are now such a feature in the landscape.

The name of the peninsula has been fruitful of controversy, being claimed by English and Gaelic writers as derived from divergent sources. Undoubtedly the true orthography of the name is Rossneath, a Gaelic term, not the modernised and more euphonious Roseneath. No doubt the latter mode of spelling is the accepted version by compilers of guide books and railway timetables, but it is repudiated by natives of the 'island', as the name is written in the old title-deeds as an unworthy concession to ignorant outsiders. One Gaelic derivation of the word is Rhosnoeth, the 'bare or unwooded promontory'; another Ros-na-choich, 'the virgin's promontory' – these being the two generally accepted terms which have gradually been corrupted into Rosneath. The latter is more generally adopted, but yet another reading gives it as Rossneveth, the 'promontory of the sanctuary'. From time immemorial there has been both a place of worship and of burial in the peninsula, in the immediate vicinity of the present church at the Clachan village. Thus the 'promontory of the sanctuary' would be an appropriate name for the now populous and frequented parish of Rosneath.

It is believed that Rosneath church was dedicated to St Modan, who lived in the sixth century, and who set out from Iona on a mission of Christianity, dwelling for a time on Loch Etive, then at the Kyles of Bute, and ending his days at Rosneath. The following quotation from the beautiful poem entitled the *Bell of St Modan's Chapel*, by Lady Elisabeth Clough Taylor, of the Argyll family, may be given here:

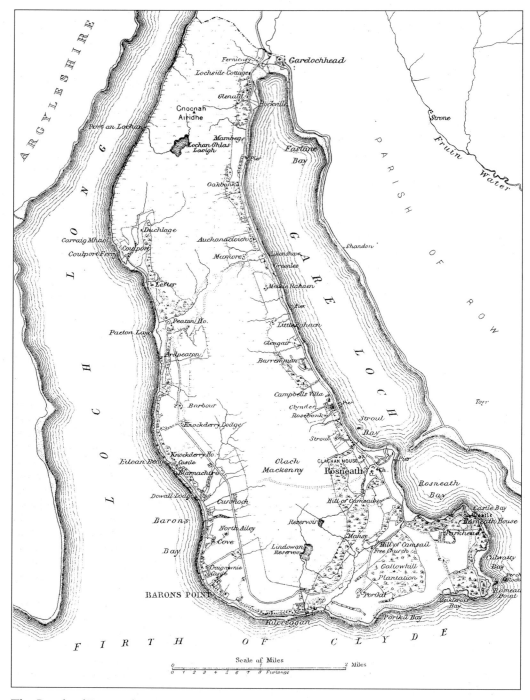

The Parish of Rosneath.

In good St Modan's ruined shrine
Once hung a golden bell,
And still Loch Etive's fishers grey
Its strange, sweet story tell –
How in the days of other years
Its healing powers were blest,
And many thronged from distant isles
In simple, trustful quest;
And none unanswered turn'd away,
But all found health and rest.

Fair is the spot Modan chose
Wherein to work and pray –
The slumberous gloom of the purple hills
O'ershadow creek and bay,
And far and wide, from yon green glen
Upon the wanderer's right,
Rises the mountain range of Mull
In ever-changing light;
While fierce and free, by Brander's Pass,
In eddying rapids wild,
The foaming Awe leaps headlong forth
From waters many isl'd.

And at his feet the ancient well
Awaking tender thought
Of all the weary, suffering souls
Its healing charm that sought –
Still feeds from the never failing depths
The murmuring mountain burn,
That low-voic'd woos the fleeting kiss
The drooping sprays of fern.
But greener woods, more smiling shores,
Wash'd by a gentler tide,
Where Cruachash and his brethren guard
The fertile vale of the Clyde,
Welcom'd the aged Saint's worn feet
To haven of repose.

And there, in memory of his name
And long life's peaceful close,
His followers rais'd the cloister'd aisles
That Fancy's feet alone
May tread again, with rapt delight,
In day dreams all her own.
Her eyes alone see 'neath sad years,
With measur'd footsteps walk,
Rossneveth's cowled monks of yore
In grave and earnest talk.

Little more than 50 years ago, along the strand of the peninsula, there was an almost unbroken verge of grass, or undergrowth of brushwood, the natural woods spreading close upon the shore about Rahne, Mambeg and Garelochhead. At Clynder there were one or two villas and some thatched houses, the shore green and grassy, where now there is a continuous row of modern mansions, trim gardens, shops, a bowling green, a pier and other indications of a teeming summer population. At that time there were no piers on the Gareloch for disembarking passengers, and when the steamers sailed up the loch, those on board had to be landed at their destinations by means of the various ferryboats at Row, Rosneath, Shandon and Garelochhead.

At this period, on landing from the old *Duchess of Argyle*, at Rosneath Ferry, the visitor would find himself on a point of land opposite Row, where the tide forms a rapid race at certain periods of its rise and fall. Often, when there is a south-west wind meeting the full force of the ebb-tide, the channel is very rough, and full of breakers. This narrow strip of water constantly changes its aspect, and according to the atmospheric phases and iridescence of the sky, the colouring of the waves is strangely varied. At the calm hour of midnight, sometimes the rushing and gurgling of the great body of water as it races and swirls on its passage through the 'Narrows' can be heard a long way off, like the sound of a cataract, even though the loch is in perfect repose. On disembarking from the steamer, 50 years ago, the only house visible was the little Rosneath Inn, which has stood in its present situation for about 100 years. Most of the stones of which the inn is built were brought from the remains of the old mansion belong to the Campbells of Carrick, which stood close to the celebrated 'Big Trees', within the Campsail woods. The former hostelry, a humble, thatched, single-storey cottage, stood a little further up, facing the bay, and the ancient road to the ferry followed the bend of the shore from Strouel bay, bordered by a row of venerable ash trees.

A short distance up the road is the Clachan of Rosneath which, even now, is a picturesque-looking row of houses, and has interesting features fast passing away. Before the erection of the

Rosneath Pier.

Ferry Inn.

The Clachan, Rosneath.

new schoolhouse and grocer's shop adjoining the row of cottages, there were old whitewashed structures, with thatched or red-tiled roofs, mellow with age and overgrown with moss and lichens. The end cottage was long known as M'Wattie's public house, one of the six which were in the parish in the days of the Revd Robert Story. The old house with its gable to the road and facing the churchyard was long used as the village school and the schoolmaster occupied the upper storey. It was for many years tenanted by the worthy schoolmaster, the late Mr John Dodds, who for fifty years taught the youth of the parish and died in 1870. In addition to the ordinary branches of knowledge imparted in Scottish parish schools, Mr Dodds taught the higher departments of mathematics, land surveying and navigation and many of his pupils (one of whom was the late distinguished Archibald Smith, Jordanhill) achieved eminence in various walks in life. His successor, the present schoolmaster, Mr William Stewart, has fully maintained the high character of the school. He has fulfilled his onerous and responsible duties to the entire satisfaction of the heritors, the School Board and community of Rosneath. Mr Stewart is of a modest and retiring disposition, but his conscientious character has gained him the respect of all. The great success that his scholars have achieved in the Bursary competitions of the county is a sure proof that the high eulogiums officially pronounced over the Clashan school are thoroughly deserved.

One of the admired features of Rosneath is the fine avenue of yew trees, which extends from the little wooden bridge over the Clachan burn, up to the old mansion at the other end, long used as a dower house by the Argyll family. It is not easy to ascertain the exact age of these stately yews, but it certainly must be well on to 200 years. In the very hottest day in summer there is ever a grateful shade under their mantling boughs, which are at many points interlaced together, and form an appropriate avenue to the ancient resting place of the dead. Sometimes the light breezes play amid their sombre sprays, with a subdued murmuring sound, like the hollow voice of the ocean. Many generations of Clachan children have voices resounding through the bosky glade. This is a favourite subject for artists and in summer they may often be observed depicting this rich sylvan scene. When the moon is full and shining down on the hoary yews, the soft shadows lie sleeping on the sward below and the vista is one full of impressive beauty. Beyond the yews are two rows of spreading lime trees which give shelter to the avenue, and whose boughs in summer resound with the hum of many bees as they gather their fragrant harvest and 'flee hame wi' lades o' treasure'.

Conjecture has been busy as to the meaning of this yew avenue and the moss-grown mansion house. It would seem that two massive stone pillars once formed the entrance at the spot where the wooden bridge over the Clachan now stands. Their foundations were seen, not long ago, by the village joiner when making some repairs. There was a tradition that a monastery had once existed where the Clachan House is placed, and when the tenant of the farm was making a drain, he came upon a quantity of massive stones, all solidly located and forming a firm foundation for a large building. The existing house has been erected at different dates, the oldest portion being next to the avenue, and it was once of much greater extent – a large wing having been pulled down about forty years ago. A little distance from the old house, along the road, you come to Strouel Well, a running stream of water that has only been known to fail on very rare occasions of extreme drought. The old road to the ferry used to run along the shore, between the beach and the venerable ash trees that overhang the strand and are, one by one, succumbing to the fury of the wintry blasts. Early in the twentieth century the road had diminished to a mere track, and has long been wholly obliterated. No doubt this was the ancient road from Glasgow to the West Highlands, by which pilgrims journeyed to Iona. It went along the loch side until Hattonburn, near the Barreman, was reached when it ran up the hillside and along the ridge of the moor for some distance, then striking down the shores of Loch Long to Coulport, from whence there has long been a royal ferry to Ardentinny.

We are now at the commencement of the various feus that have been taken off the Barremman estate, which marches with the Argyll property at the small burn beyond the

The Yew Tree Avenue, Rosneath.

Clachan House, now the site of Rosneath Primary School.

Looking north towards Stroul Bay and Clynder.

Strouel well. Feuing commenced in the year 1825, previously to which date the shore from this point to Garelochhead presented an unbroken slope of green fields and bracken-clad braes, with the exception of some thatched cottages at rare intervals. The first feu taken, in 1825, from Barremman estate, and subsequently entirely bought up, was the villa now known as Achnashie, 'Field of Peace', where the Revd Dr Macleod Campbell lived and died. It is an unpretending solid stone structure, with heavy overhanging eaves and beautifully arranged pleasure grounds, adorned with a great variety of fine shrubs and trees. Nearly opposite is the small rocky island, entirely submerged at high water, known as *Carrick-na-raon*, or 'Rock of the Seal', showing that, before the advent of the steamers, seals used to frequent the Gareloch. Passing along the shore we arrive at Clynder, where there are a few shops and a small hotel and where there used to be some rough stone houses with thatched roofs, their gables to the loch. Also at Crossowen, near where Barremman pier is placed, there was a small, old thatched farmhouse and buildings, and another similar cottage at Hattonburn. Barremman House, a plain mansion of moderate size facing the loch, is now passed; the estate for more than a century and a half was in possession of the Cumming family, and is now owned by Mr R. Thom of Canna.

A little to the north of the present house, the old mansion stands where the Cummings resided in former days, a very simple, rough-cast house of two storeys. Part of the house is of ancient build, the lower portion constructed with unhewn stones taken from the shore, interspersed with clay, and it had a thatched roof. An extra storey of more substantial architecture was added and a slated roof substituted. Over the door the names 'Patrick Cuming 1730, Mary McFarlane' are cut in the stone, and the whole has a venerable aspect, corresponding with the old ash and plane trees overhanging the wimpling burn which rushes down to the loch in small sparkling cascades. From the windows of the new mansion there is a fine prospect of the entire Gareloch. Towards the south-east the long peculiar stretch of the Row point; sometimes grey shingle, at other times merely indicated by a curved crest of broken water, while the headlands of Cairndhu and the dark promontory of Ardmore close the view. Towards the northern end of the loch, there is the lofty outline of the Loch Long range of mountains, the 'Argyll Bowling Green', and those on the Row and Shadon shores, with the ridges of Glenfruin just seen peering over the lesser heights.

On the left, up on the hillside, are seen the two farms of Little Rahane and Meikle Rahane, with their dwelling houses and steadings some way above the loch. It needs all the patience and energy which the farmers possess to enable them to overcome the unremunerative nature of their working in such exposed positions. But it is interesting to note what has been done to develop the natural capabilities of the bare hillside, and good stock has been reared on these Gareloch farms. The old farmhouse of Little Rhane – the walls of very rough stones plastered with clay and of which only a small part is now standing – used to be a favourite subject for artists, on account of its picturesque aspect. On the shore will be noticed the small village of Rahane, consisting of a few humble cottages and some villas, the first of which, Aikenshaw, was built in 1851. It is a primitive looking spot, access from the steamers being gained by the ferryboat, but its secluded situation gives it a charm in the eyes of many. The ferry house, built half a century ago, occupies the site of two older thatched structures that faced the wood, and three contiguous cottages were pulled down a few years ago. These were originally malt houses for the distillery which, many years ago, stood about a hundred yards back and of which only the faintest trace can be observed. The malt mill was a little nearer the shore, on the border of the burn into which the waterwheel projected, and used to delight the village boys with its gyrations. From here to Garelochhead the road is well shaded by the trees which grow to the very waters edge and shed their leaves in autumn into the sea, many of them fine specimens of oaks and ashes. In spring these woods, and all the fields which slope down to the road, are thickly covered with a luxuriant, beautiful growth of primroses, while the pale yellow flower also decks the mossy banks of the burns which bound down to the loch past many a shady nook. A plantation of young birch, rowan, hazel, beech, fir and other varieties of trees, clothes the hillside near Mambeg, and it is thinned for the bark at intervals of a few years. A mile beyond this, the houses of Garelochhead open to view, and the end of the parish is reached at the burn that flows down the hill from the heights above Whistlefield.

Stroul Bay. Clynder and the Barreman pier can be seen in the distance.

Returning to the Clachan of Rosneath, and proceeding in the direction of the Castle, the visitor will notice the fine old trees, chiefly of the plane and ash species, which adorn the landscape. The Mill, or Campsail Bay as it is also called, is now seen gleaming through the trees; it is one of the most beautiful inlets of water in all the Firth of Clyde, and a favourite place of anchorage for yachts of various sizes when laid up for the winter. Near the middle of the bay, an old-looking avenue gate points the way to where Campsail House once stood, formerly possessed by the Campbells of Carrick. The gateposts are covered with delicate grey lichens, and one of them has an ornamental top in the form of an acorn, but its fellow has long since disappeared. The wood beyond is a sylvan nook of rare beauty, many of the trees being old and casting a sombre shade from their mantling branches. Oaks, beeches, walnuts, Spanish chestnuts, planes and straight lofty silver firs, all combine to impress the spectator with a feeling of peace and solitude, as in some lonely forest far from the haunts of men. The bracken and ferns which clothe the ground mingle with periwinkle, wild sorrel, honeysuckle and other creepers, harmonise with the verdant retreat and the shining leaves of holly, hawthorn, sloe and ivy, thickly clustering round the rugged trunks, which gleam amid the slanting sunrays. A short walk from the old avenue gate brings the visitor in front of the two peerless silver firs, which are the special glory of Rosneath and whose fame has endured for many generations. These are two grand specimens of the fir tribe, their huge trunks, gnarled and massive, bearing all the solidity and seeming indestructibility of the granite rock, their great roots fixed deeply in the mossy soil. Probably not in Europe are there to be seen two such magnificent and venerable silver firs as these celebrated 'big trees' of Rosneath. Multitudes of visitors have been attracted to the peninsula, many from America and the Colonies, to behold these two monarchs of the forest, which for centuries have flourished in the secluded woods of the Campsail. Nearly 25ft in circumference, and 130ft in height, with immense branches springing from the great, grey, seamed stem, hoar with age and clad with lichen as the rock, these twin giants lift their verdant crests above their companions of the grove.

In winter when the whole sylvan is dazzling white with snow, only patches of bracken or thorns peer over the fleecy mass. While long streaks of snow lie on the stems of trees, or cluster in thick wreaths on their pendent boughs, the twin giants stand out with grand effect in the wintry landscape. The yews, and other dark firs beyond, seem to bring out the great trees, whose strange grouping of mighty, grey, twisted boughs, bulge and twine round one another, as though in deadly conflict they seek to rise above their fellows. Where they leave the parent stem, dark hollows and caverns are formed by their fantastic formation. All is still and quiet, the roar of the storm is hushed, the boughs are bent with the accumulated masses of snowflakes. Glancing below the drooping branches, the eye sees the swelling uplands in their silvery shroud, crowned with distant woods, arrayed in frosty garb, and overhead the misty, faintly crimsoned sky, suffused with the light of a brief winter's day. A little way off may be seen the cold, leaden-hued, calm waters of the bay. On the oozy sand are gathered some seagulls, whose screaming, querulous cries break upon the silence of the grove, and the sudden screech of the heron, in his measured flight far above, adds harsh music to the scene.

Close beside the great silver firs may be observed the foundations of the old mansion of Campsail, which once belonged to the Campbells of Carrick. Their representative, the sister of John, Duke of Argyll, and known as Lady Carrick by the Rosneath people, long lived here and was beloved for her good deeds. A sweet spot it must have been, with fine mossy sward around the ancient pile which, in the spring, is thickly carpeted with wild hyacinths and primroses, with a lovely peep through the opening branches of the bay and Helensburgh in the distance. Even now, the terraced formation of the sward indicates where the pleasure grounds had been, the old well still offers a cool draught of the limpid water and the worn flagstones of the courtyard speak of 'auld lang syne'. In the earlier part of the century, the stones of the ruinous dwelling were partly removed to build the inn at Ardencaple, near Row, and to add to the Ferry Inn at Rosneath.

Emerging from the wood by a wicket gate, between two very lofty and straight old silver firs, the road by the shore is regained and the visitor sees before him the entrance, over a low bridge, to the grounds round the castle. Lifting their dark, bushy heads above the surrounding trees are several picturesque great Scot firs, with red, rugged bark which glows warmly in the rays of the setting sun and harmonises well with the prevailing colour around. Beautiful peeps of the loch and the distant hills are gained as the visitor skirts the winding reaches of the rocky strand, and some specially venerable beech trees are seen near the old sea wall of conglomerate rock, at the spot known as 'Wallace's Leap'. It was here that the hero leaped down with his gallant steed from the summit of the rock and, though the horse was killed, Wallace succeeded in swimming across the loch to Cairndhu point. This was somewhere about the year 1297, when Wallace was contending against King Edward of England.

There is every reason to believe that the renowned warrior of Scotland did once visit Rosneath in the course of his remarkable adventures. William Hamilton of Gilbertfield, in 1721, wrote a poetic account of the hero's achievements, which was dedicated to James, Duke of Hamilton. Wallace had been engaged in one of his numerous struggles with the English, in the neighbourhood of Catheart, and was on his way to visit his friend and supporter Malcolm, Earl of Lennox. He seems to have sacked the town of Dunbarton and burnt the castle of Rosneath, which was occupied by the English, after which exploits he made his way into the strongholds of Lennox. Apparently he had been guided by one well-affected to his cause, who:

The road to Rosneath at Stroul Bay.

Clynder.

Clynder.

Directed Wallace where the South'ron lay
Who set their lodgings all in a fair low,
About their ears and burnt them stub and stow.
Then to Dunbarton cave, with merry speed,
March'd long ere day, a quick exploit indeed.
Toward Rosneath next night they past along,
Where Englishmen possest that castle strong,
Who that same day unto a wedding go,
Fourscore in number, at the least, or more.
In their return, the Scots upon them set,
Where forty did their death-wounds fairly get;
The rest scour'd off, and to the castle fled;
But Wallace, who in war was nicely bred,
He did entry to the castle win,
And slew the South'ron all were found therein.
After the fliers did pursue with speed,
None did escape him, all were cut down dead.
On their purveyance seven days lodged there,
At their own ease, and merrily did fare.
Some South'ron came to visit their good kin,
But none went out, be sure, that once came in,
After he had set fire unto the place,
March'd straight to Falkland in a little space.

Such is the account of the taking of Rosneath Castle given by Hamilton of Gilbertfield. On another of his raids against Dunbarton, Wallace was very nearly made prisoner by his relentless foes, the English. Being in a hostelry in the town, an officer and twenty-four men were sent to apprehend him, but he leapt out of the window and proceeded to assault the soldiers outside. With one or two sweeps of his terrible two-handed sword, our hero cut down the commander of the party and a dozen of his men, while the rest fled precipitately to the castle for refuge. Wallace's favourite weapon was a ponderous, long, two-handed sword which, from his great strength, he wielded with ease. Until the last few years, a rusty weapon, known as 'Wallace's Sword' was preserved in the armoury at Dunbarton Castle, and considerable indignation was aroused at its removal to the Wallace Monument at Stirling, where it now rests.

Blind Harry gives his account also of the taking and sacking of the Rosneath Castle by Wallace.

A short distance from Wallace's leap there stands the present castle, or rather palace of Rosneath, a noble building of massive construction, the work of an Italian architect, Bonomi of London, which was begun in 1803. The site is a fine one, at a greater distance from the shore than the old castle, and is said to have been selected by the famous landscape painter, Alexander Nasmyth. The former residence of the Argyll family long rested upon the point of land opposite Ardencaple. It does not seem to have been a building of any special importance or architectural merit but, about the year 1630, it was enlarged and embellished by the famous Marquis of Argyll. This mansion remained until about the beginning of the present century, when it was nearly all burnt to the ground. Upon this occasion, the old Duke of Argyll, a pious

Clynder Stores, now minus a storey, and the hotel in the background.

The northern end of the village.

Barreman Pier.

man, calmly viewed the conflagration from his castle of Ardencaple, opposite, and expressed his gratitude by saying, 'I thank my God, I have another house to go to.' An old stone, with the date 1634, carved with the cypher of the famous Marquis and his wife Margaret Douglas, is now at Inveraray castle, one of the few remains of the ancient structure. The architecture of the new castle is a mixture of Italian and Greek, massive and imposing, the splendid Ionic portico, with its lofty stone pillars, is almost unequalled in Scotland. The castle is 184ft long and 121ft in breadth, with two very handsome fronts, each adorned with fine Ionic columns, the stone being of the finest freestone from the famous Garsube quarry, near Glasgow, hewn into ponderous blocks. From the high circular tower in the centre of the building there is a grand panorama of wood, water, lawn and moor, affording endless pleasure to the spectator. Each door and window is of stately dimensions, though a large portion, both of the interior and exterior, is quite unfinished; many of the pillars with their noble capitals, and finely moulded balustrade above, never having been placed in position. Inside, the rooms are lofty and finely proportioned, one of them, the circular library under the tower, being exceedingly elegant, with decorated friezes and classic ceiling ornaments. Several family portraits adorn the public rooms, including one of the most recent, the Marquis of Lorne, in full Highland costume, and an engraving of the beautiful Miss Gunning, afterwards Duchess of Argyll.

There is an interesting old plan in the castle of the Rosneath estate, dated 1731, which shows the houses, roads and woods as they existed at that time. In this plan the castle stands back from the shore, in front of it being the 'Little Green' and to the side the 'Meikle Green', with the garden at the back, all bounded by what is called the 'new avenue'. Various crofts are marked at 'Little Ross', 'Middle Ross' and 'Meikle Ross', and several small cottages are situated at Portkill. Near Old Kilcreggan, on the opposite side of the road, is marked 'Ruins of an Old Cell', which is known locally as the 'Broken Castle', though no trace of the ruins can be seen. Near Campsail Mill there are entered an 'Upper' and 'Nether' pond, no doubt for water supply. The old house of Campsail is noted with the avenue leading straight up from the bay. Three small cottages are marked on Campsail hill, and they remained till a few years ago, when the new Clachan farmhouse was built. At the Clachan, the cruciform Kirk is put down, and the road from the castle and Campsail bay is noted as coming to an end at the Clachan village. A brickyard is situated near the present schoolmaster's house and there are two cottages at the ferry, which is called 'Clachan Point'. Going along the shore the 'Strall' spring is noted with a cottage beside it, and at 'The Clynders' there are three cottages. No houses are marked as existing on the Kilcreggan or Cove shores, but there is a pier not far from the present one. The farms of Aiden, Ailey, Knockderry and others are indicated, with a good many cottages near them, but hardly any plantations, except on the Gallowhill, and near the castle and Campsail bay.

One delightful feature is the pleasant, old-fashioned garden at the back of the castle. Its long stretches of mossy turf, quaint arrangement of laurel and heath plants, groups of flowering shrubs, graceful, drooping bushes, trimly kept walks with heavy box borders, are all vastly superior to the formal parterres now so much in vogue. The soft, mossy walks seem to allure you to stroll along, and to enjoy the scent of wallflowers, sweet peas and mignonette. There are quiet, retired nooks in which you may repose, quite secluded from observation and listen to the cooing of the wood pigeons, the lively strains of the chaffinch or the whitethroat, and the rich warbling of the mavis and the blackbird from the surrounding groves, while the songs of infancy steal over the senses, or the day dreams of youth enrapture the mind with the languor of thrilling remembrance. The shrill cry of the welcome and friendly peesweep as he lightly skims over the adjoining fields falls upon the ear and, as you advance, his graceful evolutions as he turns on the wing bring his white breast into view, pleasing to witness. The long drawn, peculiar wail of the curlew, which frequents all the shores near the 'Green Isle', is heard amid the sharper notes of the various descriptions of sea fowl which abound. Going along past Culwatty bay to the left, the dark thick wood is approached, in which is situated the heronry of Rosneath, chiefly in the midst of a number of lofty Scotch and silver firs, surrounded by a thick belt of plantation. This is a scene of sylvan repose, forming a still retreat, which the visitor would scarcely expect to meet. The screen of spruce, larch and silver firs, with rowans and beeches at intervals, is crossed by grassy glades of turf, decked in spring with a rich profusion of wild hyacinths. Only a little distance beyond is the busy, seething world of toil and commerce, with the manifold wheels of industry in ceaseless hum, while here is all the loneliness of the grove. In the spring, however, the woods resound with the harsh clamour of the herons, engaged in

Hatton Burn, formally the McGruers boatyard, now a housing estate.

Rahane.

Garelochhead from the Shore Road.

the important work of rearing their young. The nests are great unshapely masses of dried twigs, with a few tufts of coarse grass inside, and there are generally four eggs in each, of a pale green colour. While sitting on its eggs the bird will sometimes courageously defend itself if surprised by an intruder, and a blow from the long, sharp, horny bill is sufficiently severe. There were last year over eighty nests, and as you walk below the lofty trees, when the breeding season is in full swing, there is much stir and commotion overhead. The herons fly to and fro, crashing amid the boughs with their long bodies and spreading wings, many of them carrying fish in their bills to satisfy the cravings of their nestlings.

Proceeding across the fields at the back of the castle, the visitor sees the extensive pile of buildings, known locally as 'The Steeple', facing the range of steadings of the Home Farm. There is here an old threshing mill, worked by a waterwheel supplied by water brought chiefly through an underground channel all the way from Lindown reservoir, on the moor above Kilcreggan. The buildings are about 280ft in length, of massive construction and semi-Gothic architecture, and were once ornamented by a tower, 90ft in height, designed by Nasmyth of Edinburgh but which, after the great fire nearly fifty years ago, was curtailed of its lofty proportions. Originally this whole structure was intended to have been the castle stables but, for some reason or other, this was found impracticable. In front of the Home Farm rises Gallowayhill, 414ft above the sea, once completely covered with a fine plantation of fir trees, but these forty years ago were cut down by the propreitor. The view from the summit of the hill is extensive, and gives a striking idea of the diversified scenery of the Firth of Clyde. Looking towards the north, the whole of the upper part of the peninsula is seen, an undulation of purple heather and bushy bracken, while the dark mass of mountains above Loch Long, and their distant peaks, are faintly shrouded in blue haze. Many burns seam the sides of the hills round the Gareloch, whose waters reflect the fringe of trees along its shore, amid which nestle numerous villas, and the green fields above join on to the moorland ridge. The russet brown of the autumn spreads its mantle over the uplands, and the plantations on both sides are glowing with yellow and roseate tints. In the full blaze of mellow sunshine that, on an autumn day, bathes the whole loch and surrounding mountains, beautiful effects are gained by the delicate blending of the warm tints of moor, glen and sloping braes. While the edge of the nearer rugged mountain outline is sharply defined against the sides of receding peaks – which reflect the sun with brilliant lustre – a lovely soft haze envelopes the horizon, contrasting with the immediate foreground, which is strongly coloured with the purple water and the dark green of the pine forest. A white line of strand marks the upper reaches of the loch, and the tawny coloured streaks of the spreading brushwood give a variety of tints to the picture. Some of the old beech trees are seen in the castle woods, their foliage flaming with yellow and crimson, their shining, grey trunks intervening between the red Scotch firs and lordly oaks – all presenting a sylvan picture of rare beauty. Your solitude is undisturbed, for there is a considerable extent of moor round the summit of the Gallowhill, and it is difficult to realise, at certain points of the landscape, that you are so near the great bustling world of commercial enterprise of which Glasgow is the centre.

Descending the hill and rejoining the road leading over to Kilcreggan, the small hamlet of Mill of Campsail is reached. The old meal mill is a picturesque building of rubble work, 'harled' over, but long since its pristine whiteness being, in many places, thickly covered over with a soft, mossy growth like green velvet. A rich mantle of lichens covers the roof, and thick layers of downy moss overspread the stonework and eaves, while ferns have obtained a lodgement in many parts and hang their graceful fronds over the old walls. There is a date, 1752, low down on the lintel stone of the door, and another date, 1777, is cut on the stone projection at the gable, probably indicating when it was enlarged. The old wheel, with its water trough and the

The Clachan at home time, and these pictures probably say more about the changes in the area than any amount of words.

The Silver Firs – Adam and Eve.

Adam and Eve Trees, Roseneath.

Rosneath Castle, now the Caravan Park.

wooden shoot down which there trickles a tiny rivulet of water, is a favourite subject for artists. Peter McNeilage, the present miller, is a member of a family who have tenanted the mill and adjoining croft for many generations. He finds it very different from what it used to be in his father's lifetime, when the farmers in the district used to bring in their grain to be ground. His father made the first cart with wheels that came to the mill, for, before that time, the grain was brought on horses' backs in bags. The road past the mill was made about a century ago, and the millers cottage was built in 1827. A few years before, the old cottages that used to stand in the field opposite the mill across the burn, were all pulled down. In these primitive days the farmers used to dry their oats with peat fires before coming to the mill, for coals were unknown in the district. At that time there were no fanners for separating the chaff from the grain. This operation was done on the summit of the mound at the side of the millers house, known as the 'Shelling hill', where, on a breezy day, the grain and chaff were thrown into the air from bags and basket till the required result was achieved. Peter McNeilage's father and Donald Turner, the smith at the Clachan, were both baptised one Sabbath afternoon about 1792, in the open air, on the 'Shelling hill', by the Burgher minister, Mr Henderson of Kilmalcolm.

Just beyond the Mill is the Free Church, a plain building erected over the quarry from whence the stones used were extracted, but some notable men have preached within its walls, including many of those worthies who guided the fortunes of that church after the Disruption. On the hillside, beside the plantation surrounding the church, sixty years ago, there was a sweetly secluded hamlet called the Millbrae, access to which was gained by a path across the whin-clad, rocky brae, where the sheep wandered at will. Several pretty cottages were there, with gardens, fruit trees and many wild roses, some of which still remain, with broken stems and torn branches, to tell of the happy, ruddy-faced children, whose joyous voices resounded in this now silent spot. A romantic and suggestive scene, from which the spectator could survey the opening of the Gareloch, with the villas of Row beyond, looking almost like a picture on the Italian lakes, richly embowered amid trees, and the verdant crest of hills overhanging the sorrowful Glenfruin bounding the view.

Returning to the road, the traveller comes upon the broad estuary of the Clyde, with its rippling waters ploughed by many a passing vessel, and turning back, the calm land-locked Mill bay lies embosomed in trees. This bay has a charm of its own and, on a summer day, presents effects of colour, light and shade, subtle and full of beauty. The water near the shore may be dark sapphire, out in the open loch a shimmering opal, the green turf touching the strand, and the perfume-breathing beeches and oaks reflected in the waves. The sloping hills round the Gareloch close in one side of the picture, with gleaming patches of sunshine bringing into contrast the lowering and frowning mountains beyond Loch Long. Suddenly a change comes, the colours on the mobile surface of the loch are reversed, smooth bright folds seem to agitate the waters near the shore, while, further out, the depths look unnaturally calm and dark, ominous of a coming storm. Yet, here and there, tender streaks of sunshine lovingly linger between the silvery boughs of the lofty silver firs, towering above the grove. Looking round upon the broad frith, the various seaside resorts, so popular in summer, are seen on the right, dominated by the fine range of the Cowal mountains, and the rugged peaks of Arran looming grandly in the far off haze. A little way down the road on the left is the row of old cottages known as old Kilcreggan, the primitive hamlet remaining much as it was fifty years ago. In former years the tiled and the thatched cottages had a picturesque appearance, as they faced the rustling burn, which falls into the sea near the original pier; a massive structure, whose great stones still give shelter to the humble sailing craft. Before the present farm of Portkil was built, so long occupied by the Duke's chamberlain, Mr Lorne Campbell, there was an old farmhouse at Old Kilcreggan that, for many generations, had been tenanted by the Chalmers family, the last of whom died a number of years ago at Gourock. There was a small farmhouse at Portkil, a thatched building, which stood near where the present factor's house is built. Two other

Rosneath Castle.

cottages were at the top of the brae, near Portkil House but, in the various changes brought about by time, they have passed away.

At the foot of the steep brae leading to Kilcreggan pier, there stands the pretty, white cottage, embowered in flowers, where the McFarlanes, who for nearly a century worked the ferry over to Gourock, long resided, and where the venerable widow of the last ferryman still lives in serene old age. Her father and grandfather were in the Duke's service, and from the old pier, her husband's commodious wherry daily set forth for Greenock and Gourock, laden with passengers, and all sorts of farm produce, besides cattle and sheep, and brought back a miscellaneous cargo. Often great risk was run from the violent gales that would suddenly arise, and the compass had to be used when thick banks of fog enveloped the channel. It is difficult to realise that where there is now a continuous row of handsome villas all along the shore for four miles, sixty years ago there was nothing but a silent strand, laved by the clear waters of the Clyde, and the rough cart track at the foot of the heath-clad braes, all overgrown with whins, brambles and wild briar roses. One small cottage there was, situated in a beautiful alcove of rocks and rowan trees, to which the builder, whose name was Coll Turner, a member of the family long resident at the farm of Duchlage, gave the appropriate designation Craigrownie. This expressive name has since been localised by being adopted in the nomenclature of the district and *quoad sacra* parish.

One old cottage was then standing below the rocky face of the cliff above Cove pier, a humble, thatched building, long occupied as a public house by the father of the late Mr John McLean, Clachan of Rosneath, who also acted as ferryman to the opposite village of Blairmore. Going past this and crossing the Dhualt burn, which falls into the small bay of the same name, there was no dwelling on the shore road, until Peatoun mansion house, and one or two cottages beyond, were reached; an unbroken stretch extending from the farm, until you came to Coulport ferry. On the high road there were the various farms of Meikle and Little Aiden, near Kilcreggan, North and South Ailey, Knockderry and Barbour, besides some others now no longer existing. About this time the Duke of Argyll caused a carriage drive to be made along the shore, taking the place of the old cart track, rudely constructed and dangerous due to large portions of the rock protruding above the ground. Here he would drive in his stately barouche with its mighty C-Springs, and panels emblazoned with the Argyll coat of arms which, for many years had done duty both in this country and on the Continent.

Proceeding along the shore road past Cove pier, a fine prospect is opened up of Loch Long, with the dark swelling forms of the mountains rising from its deep waters, prominent among them being Cruachash, above the retired village of Ardentinney. Presently more of the purple waters of Loch Long come into view, with its slopes of fragrant heather, and the harsh cry of the grouse or black cock may be heard from the moss hag, or he may be seen skimming away in his rapid flight.

As you approach Barbour Farm, the new cemetery, made for those families resident in the peninsula who have no right of burial at Rosneath churchyard, is seen occupying a fine site, and already there are a good many graves. It is a sequestered and peaceful spot, where nature has put forth her gentle hand to soothe the sorrows of those who mourn departed friends, whose place on earth now knows them no more. Looking back, the bold headland of Knockderry stands out above the sea, an interesting spot from its being the site of an ancient Danish or Norwegian fort, hardly any trace of which now remains. As Barbour is neared, the view grows wilder, while Loch Long assumes the appearance of an inland lake, seemingly surrounded with hills. Those in the foreground bear signs of cultivation, while the mountains on the opposite shores of the loch rise steep and rugged, clothed with bracken and birchwood near the waters' edge. Ascending the hill, after crossing the Camloch burn, there is a broad expanse of moor, the distant swelling outline of the ridges beyond Loch Goil now coming into view, and the serrated peaks of the Argyll Bowling Green forming an appropriate background.

The highest point in the peninsular is easily climbed from either Peatoun or Mambeg on the Gareloch side. Its Gaelic name is *Knoch-na-Airidhe*, which, in English, may be rendered 'Hill of Shieling', and is now corrupted into Tommahara. From this moderate elevation of 717ft, it is surprising what a varied expanse of mountain, moor, craggy fell and glittering sea can be gained,

Home Farm Tower.

The Old Corn Mill.

The church.

Kilcreggan Pier.

and, on a clear day, the noble crest of Ben Cruachan may be seen. Rising above Garelochhead are the swelling outlines of the grassy mountains at the head of Glenfruin, from whence the eye ranges on to Helensburgh and to the distant braes above Kilpatrick. Opposite are the uplands of Renfrewshire, the busy ports of Greenock, Gourock and Port Glasgow, the Clpch Lighthouse, and the craggy reaches of the Aryshire coast, and following on, you gain fine views of the Cumbraes, Bute, Arran and the nearer mountains of Argyllshire. To anyone fond of studying the varied atmospheric effects visible from such a spot, according to the changes of weather, the scene from any of the higher points on the moor is full of interest. On a warm summer afternoon in June, when the sky is of a faint blue colour and the light fleecy clouds move slowly over its face, delicate changes in the aspect of the landscape will be seen. Towards the summit of the moor, the ridge of fir trees in the middle distance stands clear against the filmy sky, the gathering mist growing more dense over Loch Long and its mountains. While the outline of the peninsular behind Garelochhead is clear against the background, a thick blue haze nearly conceals the intervening glens and hollows. The fine rugged mountains about the middle of the Argyll Bowling Green loom out in solid grandeur, but those beyond Loch Goil seem very faint, until they blend with the misty haze. Cruachash, above Ardentinney, looms out by itself in rounded proportions, like a well-defined blue cloud emerging from the horizon and about to overspread the sky. The distant Ben Im, and the Cobbler above Arrochar, can faintly be traced in the nebulous haze, while a tinge of yellow suffuses the lesser heights over Glenfruin, shading away into purple all the subtle gradations of tint so impossible to depict, even by the most cunning brush. As the fleecy clouds steal over the hidden ravines, the most delicate phases of colour are observed, the fields on the loch side being of a lighter green than the pasture lands above, and the woods darker in hue where the fir trees predominate. The heather is of a brown hue, with stretches of green moss and bracken intervening, streaked with the yellow blossom of the whins. The sun's rays strike upon the beech or oak trees scattered here and there, casting their shadows upon the turf, which is decked with wild flowers. Grey walls and rocks gleam in the sunlight, and the villages and houses on the loch are seen clearly amid their verdant surroundings, the white line of the strand fringing the water. In the still depths of the purple loch the peaceful landscape is reflected, a light zeyphr ever and anon causing a faint streak of ripple to appear, with a white-winged gull skimming over the tide.

When the russet hues of autumn cast their mantle over the scene, fresh beauties appear. The mellow sunshine bathes the moor with a deep golden tint, which seems to glow amid the silvery sheen of the fir trees, and sparkles on the glistening faces of rock beside the mountain streamlets. The heather is in full bloom, and the green, mossy sward is seen in patches between the masses of abounding bracken, which has began to assume its rich brown colour. Many are the richly variegated tints of the woods which clothe the slopes of the hills, and the cornfields gleam yellow where the grain has yet to be gathered. A vapoury haze seems partially to envelope the higher mountains, and the lesser heights assume soft and rounded outlines against the blue depths of the intervening valleys. As the shades of evening steal over the still landscape, all is hushed in repose, unless the harsh, whirring cry of the grouse falls upon the ear, or the long-drawn, quavering, piping of the curlew is echoed on the sides of the ravine, and, when night darkens the scene:

> *The crisping rays, that on the water lie,*
> *Depict a paler moon, a fainter sky;*
> *While through the inverted alder boughs below,*
> *The twinkling stars with greener lustre glow*

At all seasons, and at all times of the day, there is to be seen much that will repay the closest inspection. So constantly changing is the sky, and so correspondingly varied is the colour of the Gareloch, that a series of beautiful panoramic effects reward the patient student of nature:

Kilcreggan from the shore.

Burgh Hall, Cove.

Cove Pier.

whether it be in summer, when not a cloud rests on the blue ether of the sky or is embosomed in the calm loch, with all nature quivering in the hot, impalpable haze; or in winter, with a soft shroud of snow enveloping mountain, field and garden alike, the picture is radiant with loveliness. Spring has its own peculiar elements of beauty; the first suffusion of the glow of mingling colour, which afterwards, pervades the spot. Autumn's rich mosaic flames over wood and brake, and the deep crimson of the setting sun flushes over sky and strand. At times, the sun's horizontal rays, just before the luminary is sinking behind the Loch Long hills, catch upon the upper ranges of fir trees, investing them with an exquisite pearly grey hue. And, in winter, while all the ground is robed in snow, there is a solemn stillness that awes the feelings of the solitary wayfarer. The loch is chill and leaden in aspect, the fields and moors have all landmarks obliterated beneath the snowy mantle, the trees are powered with hoarfrost, their black branches are set off by silvery rime. If it is morning, as the early sun begins to suffuse the sky, then the graceful forms of the trees are traced out in fleecy indistinctness. As the sunrays grow warmer, a yellow tinge spreads on the woods above but, lower down, all is coldly grey. Nearer to the beholder the pale frosted boughs are traced against the horizon in a delicate fretwork, and showers of snow, like ocean spray, fall from the evergreens as the startled wood pigeon rushes from his perch. By the moonlight, the scene is only deepened and intensified, the snow is more ethereal, the trees more ghostly, and the hills more unreal in their dusky outline. Each far-off peak gleams faintly against the wan firmament in the cold glitter of the stars.

Atmosphere and cloud effects of singular and varied beauty are to be observed at various seasons, some of the finest of them in the early hours of a summer morn, or about midnight when the days are longest. It would need all the word painting of a Ruskin to do justice to such a scene. Sometimes great masses of billowy clouds are heaped above the Loch Long mountains and, as the early sunrays play upon the shifting surface, subtle gradations of colour can be marked. A bright patch of clear sky is opened up from time to time, and it is difficult to distinguish the rugged outlines of the hills from the clearly developed lines of clouds traced against the horizon. There is, in summer, sometimes a lovely effect of deep purple in the colours of the cloudbanks resting on the mountain ridges, and innumerable islands seem to float in a golden sea. This cloudbank becomes all the denser and darker as the clear border of the sky is more and more reflected in the still waters of the loch. Great mountain precipices and vast crags seem toppling over in the moving cloudland overhanging the waters. The pale green of the young bracken is in strong contrast with the purple clouds, and light streamers of mist curl themselves round the fir plantations.

At the height of the summer, when there is hardly any night, and the faint flush of a new day is fast tingeing the sky, a still and impressive scene of beauty is presented to the eye. A dark mass of clouds rests on the highest ridges, while away at either end of the horizon light is reflected in the placid loch. The foreground is of an indefinite hue, the trees and moorland ghostly and ill-defined, the murky atmosphere lending faint colour to the picture. The great and dominate feature is the dark shroud overhanging the distant hills, intensely gloomy and seemingly charged with presaging woe. An oppressive languor pervades the atmosphere, even at the hour of early dawn, and all nature is hushed in preternatural repose.

Moonlight on the Gareloch has always a beautiful effect, owing to the rugged outlines of the mountains against the canopy of heaven, and the smooth unbroken surface of the water, which reflects the stars in their lustrous sheen. To view the scene in all its weird and ghostly loveliness, a visit to the summit of the Gallowhill, the high ground at the end of the Rosneath peninsula, will well repay the walk. It is a lonely spot, but it commands the view far down the Clyde, as

Knockderry House, now an hotel.

well as the Gareloch, and the hills near Helensburgh and Cardross. On such an evening the horizon immediately above the Loch Long mountains is of pale green, against which the purple peaks are sharply outlined and the trees on the crest of the nearer slopes are softly pencilled against the luminous sky, as if they were but shadows. The Arran Mountains seem like dark clouds, but the contour of the hills on the Argyllshire coast is more clearly defined. The broad Firth glows in the moon's lustre, and the lights of the various towns twinkle along the dark line of the strand. Ardmore Point, in deep shadow, reaches far into the sea, and faintly visible in the distance is the great mass of Dunbarton Rock. In the near foreground are the woods around Rosneath Castle, and the lamps of Row are reflected in the calm waters of the bay. Hushed is the night breeze on the solitary moor, but the cry of an owl arises from the old fir trees, and sounds strangely in keeping with the solemn stillness around. Overhead, the blue, glittering stars scintillate with gem like effulgence in the opaque, purple firmament. An hour and a spot calling for reverent contemplation, as the musing spectator views the pale picture, so delicately lambent in the wan rays of the moon.

Standing on the hill on such a peaceful evening, watching the gleaming silver ripple on the broad estuary and the long avenues of lights shining in stillness on the opposite strand – a belt of fire beside the dimly purple water – the mind of the lonely stranger must respond to the impressive associations of the spot. Yon steep-rising town, with many a tall chimney pointing to the star spangled sky, is the place where a great but modest man of genius, who first gauged the gigantic power of steam, saw the light of day. He solved the problem of how to blend the two opposing forces of water and fire, and summoned into being the terrific energy of steam. The genius of Watt so regulated the mighty throbbings of the imprisoned giant within that iron cylinder that the transmitted energy sufficed to drive the ponderous vessel through the mountainous billows of the Atlantic. At the summons of the magicians' wand, the spirits which lay dormant in those antagonistic elements, brought together in auspicious union, have evolved a power far transcending the fabled Cyclops of the Grecian poet. Seated at his workshop, just across the gently heaving water, the brain of the unknown mechanician, solved the problem which was to add a new-born motor to nature, and created novel possibilities in the scientific world whose might would be felt throughout succeeding ages. Contrasting the puny results of the dynamics of the past century with the marvellous achievements of the modern steam engine, it seems almost as though one looked upon the feeble rushlight in some lonely midnight cell, and next morning beheld all rising effulgence of the rolling sun in its glory, lighting up the firmament with approaching meridian splendour.

Turning round in the moon's rays, the lights of Helensburgh shine out against the opposite side of the estuary, and in the imagination appears the humble wheelwright, whose prophetic insight into the future of steam navigation enabled him to conjure up a vision of great transatlantic steamers, ploughing their way through the green and billowy ocean. Henry Bell lived for many years in Helensburgh, a man of fine inventive skill, and destined to adorn a niche in the temple of science. He patiently matured his schemes for using the infant force of the steam engine, and impelling his vessel against the solid impact of the ocean waves. Nor did he seek to enlist the favouring gale in guiding his ship over the waste of waters, the opposing blast had to yield to the overmastering strength of steam, and the mariner could face even the raging tempest with the assured hope of success. The crested Atlantic rollers would no longer daunt the aspiring traveller searching for the far-off parts of the world, and the anxious merchant could send away his argosies, freighted with the rarest products of the loom, to swell the stream of commerce on the banks of the swift rolling Ganges, or amid the palm girt islands of the Malay Archipelago.

Where the heavy-timbered, painted galleys, with the rude warriors from the North Sea, slowly and cumbrously made their way up the waters of the Clyde, their carved prows and long bending oars toiling through the waves, now may seem the mighty iron-clads, bearing aloft those guns whose discharge shakes the adamantine rocks, with self-impelled, resistless way, moving majestically to their appointed place. Their shadows fall athwart the watery channel,

Cove from the foreshore.

and they lie each one at anchor destined, perchance, to destroy the fell usurper's power, or bear the 'meteor flag' of Britain to victory in a far-off conflict, whose echoes shall one day reverberate amid the 'cloud cap'd towers' and sun-girt palaces of some hostile fortress. All these now sleeping shores, when dawn begins to steal over the mountain brow, will awake to the busy hum of the toiling masses and the whirring wheels of commerce, and how vast is the debt of gratitude which they owe to that illustrious man, whose discovery was fraught with incalculable blessings to the human race.

Down these waters had sailed, from nearly isolated lofty rocky fortress, whose rounded outline is faintly indicated amid the misty exhalations from the Vale of Leven, some of Scotland's monarchs on their voyages in quest of glory and success in love and war. Amongst them yon hapless queen, around whom gathers an environment of crime and woe, while warriors and statesmen, famed in the annals of their country, swelled the ranks of her attendants. Here, too, the warrior king of Scotland was wont to sail in his galleys of pleasure, reclined amid the companions he loved, and who stood by him on many a field of gore, and who sought retirement in his declining years by the verdant banks of the smoothly flowing Leven. And up the winding Firth, in their humble sailing craft, there came from the shore of Ireland and the Western Isles, those pious and holy men bringing as their blessed evangel, 'Peace on earth and goodwill towards men'. A rich blending of ancient story, woven into one long drawn chain of mellowing reminiscences, over which the mind and fancy might well linger in pensive reverie.

Tis a picture in memory distinctly defined
With the strong and impershing colours of mind.

The never-dying interest which attaches to all that proceeded from the magic pen of Sir Walter Scott renders the latter portion of the *Heart of Midlothian* of special import to those who seek to connect the romantic incidents of each stirring narrative with the actual surroundings and history of the scene in which they were laid. In almost all the tales of the 'Wizard of the North,' his descriptions of scenery, and peculiarities of the people and territory of which he is treating, prove that he himself had gone over the ground with the view of giving graphic touches worthy of the master. But there is good ground for believing that in the pathetic tale of the hapless Effie Deans, and her noble sister Jeanie, Sir Walter trusted to memory, or to information derived at second hand. To begin with, in the story, Rosneath is throughout spoken of as an island, and many of his readers rise from the perusal of the fortunes of the Deans family, fired with the wish to inspect the beautiful isle, where so much that is of thrilling interest is concentrated. Not that Sir Walter is singular in the idea he had conceived of the insular form of Rosneath, for in old title deeds of the local families it is sometimes mentioned as the 'isle', and, in former days, colloquially it was spoken of as 'the island'. Most readers are familiar with the beautiful story of the *Heart of Midlothian*, which largely turns upon the powerful influence with the King and Queen wielded by the great chief of the Clan Campbell, the Duke of Argyll. Following the fortunes of the simple and guileless Jeanie Deans who had, after surmounting many difficulties, reached London on foot, she is found in the library of his Grace, who arranges that she should have a private interview with Queen Caroline, in order that she may plead for a pardon for her sister Effie. Sir Walter thus describes the character of John Duke of Argyll and Greenwich:

Soaring above the petty distinctions of faction, his voice was raised, whether in office or opposition, for those measures which were at once just and lenient. His high military talents enabled him, during the memorable year 1715, to render such services to the House of Hanover as, perhaps, were too great to be either acknowledged or repaid. He had employed, too, his utmost influence in softening the consequences of that insurrection to the unfortunate gentlemen whom a mistaken sense of loyalty had engaged in the affair, and was rewarded by the esteem and affection of his country in an uncommon degree.

Coulport.

Shandon Hydro.

Rhu (Row) Narrows.

Cottages at the foot of Whistlefield Brae.

This powerful nobleman's influence with the Queen secured Effie's pardon, and the thread of the story is soon transferred to Scotland, and more particularly to Rosneath. Having elicited from Jeanie in her open artless way the information as to her own life and her own simple love passages, in which Reuben Butler bore a part, the Duke sought to do his best to bring to fruition the hopes which the lovers had ventured to entertain in their own unsophisticated way. He also wished to discharge the debt of gratitude under which his ancestor lay to the grandfather of Reuben, who had been the means of saving his life on one occasion in the Civil War, and he resolved to present Jeanie's lover with the living of the Parish of Knoctarlitie, which was in his Grace's gift. Jeanie's father 'Douce Davie Deans' had, unknown to the former, been placed by the Duke in charge of a new farm in the Rosneath. It was therefore arranged that she should travel to Scotland, under the charge of a discreet attendant of the Argyll family, along with a somewhat timorous and extremely voluble English dairywoman, by name Mrs Dolly Dutton. Readers of the novel know well how they proceeded on their journey and finally reached their destination at the Duke's residence in Dunbartonshire.

The following is the description which Sir Walter gives of the district in which the lot of the Deans family was now cast:

> The islands in the Firth of Clyde are of exquisite, yet varied beauty. Rosneath, a smaller isle, lies much higher up the firth, and towards its western shore, near the opening of the lake called the Gare-Loch, and not far from Loch Long and Loch Seant, or the Holy Loch, which wing from the mountains of the Western Highlands to join the estuary of the Clyde. In these isles the severe frost winds which tyrannise over the vegetable creation during a Scottish spring, are comparatively little felt. Accordingly the weeping-willow, the weeping-birch, and other trees of early and pendulous shoots, flourish in these favoured recesses in a degree unknown in our eastern districts. The picturesque beauty of the island of Rosneath, in particular, had such recommendations, that the Earls and Dukes of Argyll, from an early period made their occasional residence, and had their temporary accommodation in a fishing or hunting lodge, which succeeding improvements have since transformed into a palace.

The Pier, Cove.

Cove Pier from the north.

Bibliography

W.C. Maughan, *The Annals of Garelochside*, 1897.

Other local books that readers may find interesting:

Irving, *The Book of Dumbartenshire Vols 1 and 2*, 1879.

C.L. Warr, *The Call of the Island*.

F.M. Crum, *The Isle of Rosneath*, 1948.

D. Royal, *United States Navy Base Two*, 2000.